I Could Chew on This

....

AND OTHER POEMS BY DOGS

I Could Chew on This

....

AND OTHER POEMS BY DOGS

BY FRANCESCO MARCIULIANO

CHRONICLE BOOKS

SAN FRANCISCO

Library of Congress Cataloging-in-Publication Data
Marciuliano, Francesco.
    [Poems. Selections]
    I could chew on this : and other poems by Dogs / Francesco Marciuliano.
        pages cm
    ISBN 978-1-4521-1903-8
    1. Dogs--Poetry. I. Title.

PS3613.A7348I22 2013
811'.6--dc23
                        2012042336

The following images copyright © iStockphoto.com/photographer: bortonia, 2 (bone); luoman, 2
(typewriter); herkisi (frames), 5, 11, 44, 49, 61, 67, 76, 93, 111; dageldog, 13, 40; SuperflyImages,
14; Palto, 16; edurivero, 19; MoniqueRodriguez, 20; chictype, 23; Leontura, 27; SVM, 28; tderden,
31 (dog); broken3, 32; snapphoto, 34; Shershel, 36; robh, 38-39; m.p.imageart, 42; golfladi, 44;
membio, 49; EduardoLuzzatti, 50; tomeng, 53; -aniaostudio-, 56; standby, 61; paule858, 62; Jot,
64-65; Wavetop, 67; herreid, 68; hnijjar007, 73; Floortje, 75; Fenne, 76; deviousrlm, 81; craftvision,
82; ProjectB, 84; cillay, 86-87; DebbiSmirnoff, 91; bit245, 92; ruthrose, 97; sentido_fotografia, 99;
cmannphoto, 100; Juanmonino, 103; ZoneCreative, 105; oddrose, 106; patty_c, 108; Nadeika, 111.
The following images copyright © Shutterstock.com/photographer: Kathie Nichols, 10-11; mareku-
liasz, 21 (stamp); Jiggo_thekop, 31 (background); Denis Hsn Photography, 47; SeDmi, 55; Cathy
Keifer, 89. 5 copyright © Francesco Marciuliano. 6 copyright © Renee Stockdale/Kimball Stock.

Manufactured in China

Designed by **Emily Dubin**

10 9 8 7

Chronicle Books LLC
680 Second Street
San Francisco, California 94107
www.chroniclebooks.com

Dedicated in cherished memory to Panda,

the sweetest, most loving,

perhaps poetically gifted

(we like to think)

dog a family could ever have.

CONTENTS

.... 🐾 ....

INTRODUCTION

·············· 🐾 ··············

Dogs have never been shy about expressing their emotions. When they're happy, they wag their tails. When they're nervous, they wag their tails. And when they're suffering from ennui, they wag their tails—a slow, mournful sway scored to a lone piano—as their soul remains as empty as the food dish they devoured before tearing into a Hefty bag replete with uncertainty and pizza rolls.

But while dogs may wear their hearts on their sleeves (especially when forced to wear a poncho), people have never truly known what goes on in their minds. Until now, that is. Thanks to an unprecedented—and unaccredited—writing program, dogs everywhere are exposing their true inner lives through the power of poetry. From their rich experiences indoors to a wealth of wisdom gathered outside, from their unbreakable bond with their owners to the way their hearts shatter whenever they're placed inside a purse, these canine verses reveal why dogs keep sniffing, why dogs keep running, and why dogs keep staring at you until you just break down and reveal state secrets you never even knew you knew.

The dogs are trying to reach out to you. They want you to know what they ponder, what they desire, and what you can do with those rain boots you just bought them. So read their poems. See the world as they do. And maybe the next time your furry friend is neck-deep in trash, you'll gently pet his head and say, "I understand now. I do. But no one has ever found what they were looking for at the bottom of three pounds of partially thawed rolled pizza. Trust me, I know."

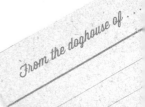

From the doghouse of . . .

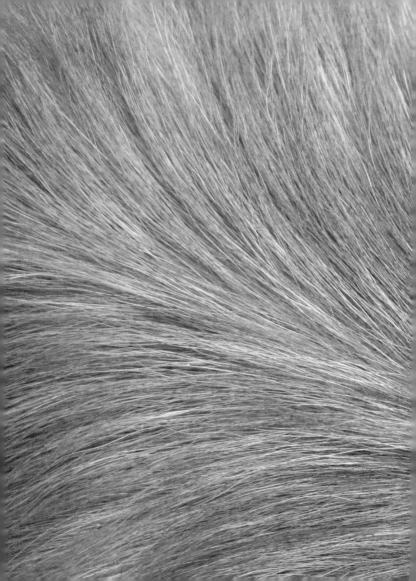

INSIDE

We were wolves once

Wild and wary

Then we noticed you had sofas

DOG DICTUM

I Lose My Mind
When You Leave the House

The plants are torn

The garbage strewn

The wires chewed

The couch and I had a fight

Your bed is soaked

Your liquor spilled

Your TV smashed

Your laptop no longer has any vowels

There's a smartphone in the toaster

There's a toaster in the toilet

There's a toilet in the hallway

There's underwear in my mouth

I went places I should never go

I saw a side of myself I should never see

I said things to the cat I can never take back

So please don't ever leave again

I've Been Watching

Maybe you should shift to your left
Maybe you should move your knee
Maybe you should go a little slower
Maybe you should stay there a little longer
Maybe you should try talking this once
Maybe you should never say that again
Maybe you should play dress-up
Maybe you don't know how to act like a pirate
Maybe you don't want my advice
Maybe this is not the time or place
But I've been watching you two every night
For the past six years
So maybe I know a little something
   about making love.

On the TV

Whenever I hear
A dog bark on the TV
I bark and bark and bark
But the dog on the TV
Never barks back
Probably because a lot of celebrities
Are really stuck up

Hoarding

Ooo! A remote! I'll take it!

Ooo! A sponge! I'll take it!

Ooo! A shirt! I'll take it!

Ooo! A plastic bottle! I'll take it!

Ooo! A USB drive! I'll take it!

Ooo! Carpet padding! I'll take some!

Ooo! Underpants! They're in my mouth now!

Ooo! A ... thing! That's going under the bed!

You may think this hoarding is a problem

You may think that I need some help

But I prefer to see it as

  a very gradual robbery

So hand over your left slipper

Dance of Joy

· · · · · · · · · · · · · ·

This is the dance I do for you, do for you
This is the dance I do for you
As you get my can of food
This is the twirl I do for you, do for you
This is the twirl I do for you
As you open my can of food
This is the leap I do for you, do for you
This is the eight-foot vertical leap
  I do for you
As you stop serving my food to answer
  the phone
This is me running in a sheer panic,
  wild panic
This is me running in desperate,
  gasping, blind panic
As you continue to talk on the phone

THIS IS ME LOSING MY [censored] MIND

MY [censored] BRAINS, MY [censored] COOL

THIS IS ME WONDERING WHAT THE [censored]

COULD BE SO [censored] IMPORTANT

THAT YOU'RE STILL ON THE [censored] PHONE

This is me realizing I was howling out loud,

  really loud

And that perhaps I overreacted

  just a little

And so this is me eating the food

  you give to me, always give to me

Going Somewhere?

I know this routine

The gathered clothes

The miniature toiletries

The bag with wheels, handle, and zipper

I know what happens next

The short trip

The long trip

The time away from me

I know there's nothing left but

The farewell licking

The final whining

The last minute burying of all your ID

Like I said, I know this routine

And this time Delta's leaving without you

Subterfuge

. . . .

A nudge of nose

A slight of hand

And within a moment it is done

I appear by your side

Right there for the drop

And another mission is complete

As spies in the night

As agents in the field

And as couriers we must not be caught

Then something goes wrong

Then I hawk up a bone

Then twelve pieces of meat

And then that napkin I ate without thinking

A resource is lost

A network undone

And alas, there will be no more table scraps
  tonight

Buffet

Okay

All right

Hold on

Just another second

There

I've successfully digested

A dirty diaper

Really, the things you people throw out

In a garbage pail at nose level

But hey

I'm always up for a challenge

Nothing Seems to Work

. . . .

I use my teeth

I try my paw

I whine a lot

I walk in circles

But nothing seems to work

Then, with a twist of your wrist

You turn the doorknob

And that's when I finally realize

You're a wizard

Bored

. . . .

I get so bored

So very bored

Being all alone

Stuck inside this house

House

House

House

House

House

Which explains why

I shoved my head inside this jar

And everything has an echo

Now does anyone have any Vaseline?

Where Are You?!?

. . . .

I was so worried

I was so scared

I thought that I had lost you

And the life that we both shared

I searched through the entire house

From the basement to the attic

The living, dining, and bedrooms

Even the trash cans, because I was frantic

Up and down the staircase

Back and forth across the halls

In and out through every door

Louder and louder were my calls

I had given up every hope

I had given in to despair

I had given the bad news to the pet cat

Who gave me a look before re-licking her hair

But just when all seemed lost, I found you
And it gave my heart a rush
To see you sitting—startled, but alive and well
So if you don't mind,
   I'll just stay here until you flush

Season's Barkings!

FROM OUR LITTER TO YOURS

Holiday Card

Two little sweaters

Two big smiles

Two happy pets

Together

Too cute

Then the photo is taken

The cat swipes at my face

And we mail out our annual lie

   of family bliss

Bath

· · · · · ·

Bath!

I'm taking a bath!

Hey! I'm taking a bath!

I'm taking a soapy

Sudsy

Oh so foamy

Big ol' bath!

Just thought you should know

That I'm taking a bath!

Now I'm going to shake

Now that feels so good

Now if you'll excuse me

I really should run back upstairs

To finish my bath

Bath!

Judgment Call

. . . .

I don't know what to do

I don't know where to go

I don't want to be wrong

I just want to be good

But I know they are waiting

And I want to succeed

So I pick a spot on the newspaper

Only to pee on the arts section

And now everyone thinks I'm a philistine

DOORBELL!

. . . .

THAT WAS THE DOORBELL!

SOMEONE RANG THE DOORBELL!

SOMEONE'S AT THE DOOR!

I CAN HEAR THEM AT THE DOOR!

I CAN'T WAIT TO SEE WHO'S AT THE DOOR!

OH PLEASE LET ME SEE WHO'S AT THE DOOR!

WHY ARE YOU TAKING ME

AWAY FROM THE DOOR?!

WHY AM I BEING PUT IN THIS ROOM

AWAY FROM THE DOOR?!

OH, MAGICAL, MYSTERIOUS PERSON

WHO RINGS OUR DOORBELL!

ONE DAY WE SHALL MEET!

Sympathy

. . . .

I'm not expecting

Any sympathy

I'm not asking

For any pity

I'm not seeking

Any condolences

I'm not hoping

For any sorrow

But that giant roast

You were going to have for your party

Before I just ate it

Still isn't sitting right in my belly

So maybe I am expecting

A small sense of gratitude

For saving you from this pain

I Dropped a Ball

I dropped a ball in your lap

It's time to play

I just put a ball in your lap

So it's time to play

See that ball I placed in your lap?

That means it's time to play

You can have your emergency appendectomy

Any other day

But I dropped a ball in your lap

And now it's time to play

OUTSIDE

· · · · · · · · · · · ▪━▪ · · · · · · · · · · · ·

Best not to ask

"What is it?"

Until you finish

Rolling in it

DOG MANTRA

Unleashed

. . . .

I'm free!

I'm free!

I'm free!

I'm free!

I'm free!

I'm free!

I'm lost.

Across the Park

. . . .

I ran all the way across the park
I ran as fast as I could
I ran right into bird poop
Which is in no way as good as dog poop
And I looked and looked and looked for it
I started doubting my abilities
I started questioning my sanity
I started seeing if the bird poop tasted any good
I even thought a squirrel must have taken it
Which is why I chased them all for half an hour
And then I came all the way back across the park
Panting and wheezing and pelted with nuts
Only to find you PRETENDED to throw the ball?!

Alpha

· · · · · · ·

Scruffles is our leader

Scruffles is our king

Scruffles is the captain of our pack

Scruffles' praises we each sing

Scruffles is who we always follow

Scruffles shows us all the way

Scruffles led us to an abandoned factory

In the middle of freaking nowhere

And not even a fun abandoned factory

But one that made belt buckles

Now Scruffles is why we're all thinking

We really need some sort of voting process

Or at least a system of checks and balances

Purse Dog

Just because

I'm carried around in a purse

High above the dirty ground

Does not mean

I'm less of a pet

Less of a dog

Less of a true canine

It just means

I think I can fly

And that I know

What lipstick and loose change taste like

Can You Smell That?

. . . .

I smell the air

I smell the dew

I smell that rock

I smell your shoe

I smell the leaves

I smell a slug

I smell the dirt

I inhale a bug

I smell the grass

I smell the grass

I smell each and every

Blade of grass

I smell a butt

Oh hey, it's Lou!

I smell frustration

Oh hey, that's you!

I sniff, I snort, I even snuff

And with every scent my nose does sing

But you say quite sharply

  it's been two hours

So let's smell what the next foot

  of our walk does bring

Splash

. . . .

I GOT IT! I GOT IT! I GOT IT!

I'm wet

I GOT IT! I GOT IT! I GOT IT!

I'm soaked

I GOT IT! I GOT IT! I GOT IT!

I'm drenched

I GOT IT! I GOT IT! I GOT IT!

I'm begging you

Please stop skipping stones across the lake

Because clearly I don't know

When not to chase something

Chasing Cars

. . . .

I'm getting closer

I'm picking up speed

I'm catching up

I'm almost upon it

Yes!

I did it!

Now I can finally read

What that bumper sticker says

Oh, apparently there's a presidential election

In 2004

Really, dude, update your car decals

Sheepdog

. . . .

You go to the left

You go to the right

You stand next to me

And done

I've successfully herded

All your children by instinct

And in order of attractiveness

Oh, and tell Billy I'm sorry

But I'm sure he'll grow into his nose

Outside the Store

. . . .

I don't very much like

Being tied up outside the store

I don't very much like

Looking as if I were forgotten

I don't very much like

Having to make small talk with passing dogs

I don't very much like

How it looks as if it might rain

How it feels as if you've been gone forever

How the only thing I have to read

Is the same parking sign again and again

I don't very much like

That you tied me up outside the store

Which is why I'm not going to the bathroom

Until we get home

Little One

. . . .

WHO ARE YOU LOOKING AT, HUH?!

WHO ARE YOU LOOKING AT?!

YOU THINK I'M AFRAID OF YOU, HUH?!

YOU THINK I'M AFRAID OF YOU?!

YOU'RE NOT SO BIG!

YOU'RE NOT SO TOUGH!

C'MON, I DARE YOU!

C'MON, I'LL DESTROY YOU!

THAT'S IT, JUST WALK AWAY!

GO ON, JUST WALK AWAY!

Oh please, just walk away

Oh God, that dog was a monster

Oh man, I need to relax

Or at least switch to herbal tea

Another Bag

Love

True, unbridled love

Is looking at what I just did

On the sidewalk

And then picking it up in a bag

I can only imagine as a treasured keepsake

Wow, the collection you must have by now

Chain Reaction
. . . .

Late one night

I step out in the yard

And bark

Then the neighbor's dog barks

Then his neighbor's dog barks

And so it goes

House to house

Street to street

Town to town

State to state

Coast to coast

Until the very last dog

Tallies up those barks

And that's how we elect our president

NORTH DOGOT

DRIVER'S LIC

**FIFI PU
123 KII
DOGVI**

Date of B
11-21-201

Breed
Terrier

Height
0-10

ISSUED

DOG9876543210

Next Car Over

. . . .

Hey, there's a dog in the next car over
There's a dog in that car by the light
Hey, dog!
Dog!
Okay, dog, let me—
I'm just trying to—
Please stop interrupt—
If I can get in one—
FINE, DOG! IS THAT HOW YOU WANT IT?!
YOU LIKE SOMEONE TALKING OVER YOU?!
HUH?! HUH?! HUH?! HUH?! HUH?! HUH?!
And now he's gone
Sigh
This is why I never make friends

King of the Mountain

I am king of this icy mountain!

I am ruler of this wintry hill!

I am conqueror of this frozen peak!

So I lift my leg to claim my throne

So I notice the ice starts to melt

So I fall right through this huge snowdrift

So if you could come dig me out

I would very much like

To go back to my warm, dry home

Look at Me!

. . . .

"Look at me!" I bark

As I run around the dog park

And you point at me with pride

"Look at me!" I bark

As I play with other dogs

And you give me a happy wave

"Look at me!" I bark

As I wag my tail with glee

And you show me a great big smile

"Look at me!" I bark

As I shove my nose so far up another dog's
   ass

I'm almost looking out its mouth

And you become fascinated with your shoes

BY YOUR SIDE

·········· ▰ ··········

People need a lot of reassurance

So show them that you love them

And never wince when they sing

DOG PRECEPT

Wingman

I wag my tail

I tilt my head

I give a little wink

I flash my smile

I show my belly

I give a little lick

I do it all

From sit to speak

To attract women far and near

Then you chime in

With something about "fan fiction"

And I realize we're going to die alone

Time
· · · · · ·

Where did you go?!

Where have you been?!

Do you know how long you've been gone?!

Three hours!

Or fifteen minutes

Or six months

The point is

I've been waiting at that door

For eighteen straight years

And every one of those twelve seconds killed me

If You Got Lost

. . . .

If you got lost I would find you

If you got hurt I would help you

If you got trapped I would save you

If you got abducted by aliens

I would cripple their ship's computer system

By uploading a virus—somehow

For you I would swim across the deepest ocean

For you I would jump across the widest chasm

For you I would race across the biggest country

So now that you know

All that I would gladly do for you

Maybe you can do something for me

And give me a braver name than "Wiggles"

And Then Our Eyes Lock

. . . .

And then our eyes lock

And then the world stops

And then I realize

Man, I'm really wrapped around your leg

Man, I'm really going to town

Man, I'm clearly not stopping

So believe me when I say

Our next twenty minutes together

Will be the most awkward of my entire life

Lassie

. . . .

How come

With just a few barks

Everyone can understand

That Lassie is saying

Timmy fell down the well

But with my endless whining and gnawing

You can't understand

That I am saying

I'd rather the earth swallowed me whole

Than go out in public wearing this raincoat

Six Ways

There are six ways
To say my name
One, when you are happy to see me
Two, when you are afraid you lost me
Three, when you instruct me
Four, when you scold me
Five, when you nuzzle me
And six, when you catch me
Eating another dog's poo
Although that last one
Just seems to involve a lot of
   screaming and nausea

Never Learn

. . . .

Why

Why

Why

Do I think that

Every time you tell me to get in the car

You're finally taking me to the

Hole-Digging Shoe-Chewing

   Butt-Sniffing Ball-Licking

Amusement Park

And not for my shots

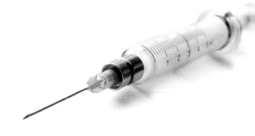

When I See You

. . . .

When I see you head for the kitchen

I know it's time for my dinner

When I see you walk to the yard

I know it's time for us to play

When I see you go to the car

I know it's time for a drive

When I see you turn on the TV

I know it's time for my head on your lap

And when I see you climb into bed

I know it's time for my walk

Kisses

· · · · · · · ·

I lick your face when you bend down to pet me

I lick your hand when it hangs off the chair

I lick your palm when you nuzzle my chin

I lick your feet when you're sound asleep

I lick your nose

I lick your legs

I even lick your eye

(When I try to lick your cheek)

I lick and lick and lick you

All over and over again

Because I love you

And because one day you're going to fall

Into a vat of taco meat

And frankly I don't want to miss out

Sit

· · · ·

You want me to sit?

You'd like me to sit?

You need me to sit?

You're asking me to sit?

You're saying louder for me to sit?

You're yelling for me to sit?

You're begging for me to sit?

You're pleading for me to sit?

You say the word "sit"

Like I have any clue what it means

But I love your enthusiasm

And so I jump up and down with joy

   for the both of us

Dog Breath

. . . .

Smell my breath

Go ahead, smell my breath

Really get in there

Right up to my mouth

And smell my dog breath

Can you guess what it is?

Can you tell what I ate?

Because I swallowed it so fast

Before it could escape

And frankly, I'm curious to find out

No Longer Together

My two people no longer share a bed

So now one mattress is far too big

My two people no longer share a home

So now one smell I cannot find

My two people no longer share a life

So now one person I don't see much at all

My two people no longer are together

And I can't help but wonder

If it's because of something I did

Or maybe that Turkish rug I soiled

Lapdog

. . . .

A lapdog

Is any dog

Who wants to be really close

So stop your muffled screams

And your cracking pelvis

And just celebrate the fact

That this mastiff loves you so

Special Word

· · · · · · · · · · · · · ·

There's a special word

We dogs have

To express our great pleasure

Upon seeing our favorite person

It's "bark"

But be careful

For "bark"

Also means 742,000 other things

So it's all really about the context

CHAPTER

HEAVY THINKING

··············· ▬ ···········

It's not easy being a dog

Especially when your person

Thinks you look good in hats

D O G   M U S I N G

The Naming
. . . .

Give me something strong

Give me something powerful

Give me something noble

Give me something memorable

Give me something

To carry through all my years

With back straight and chin held high

But then you ask your three-year-old daughter

"Why don't you name the new puppy?"

And I'm so screwed that I could cry

The Cone

· · · · · · · · · ·

Thanks to the cone

I can't gnaw at my stitches

Thanks to the cone

I can't turn my head

Thanks to the cone

I can't navigate hallways

Thanks to the cone

I get stuck in doorways

Thanks to the cone

I misjudge the stairs

Thanks to the cone

I get claustrophobic when I bend

  for my food dish

Thanks to the cone

I go deaf when I bark

Thanks to the conc

Our every game of catch turns into basketball

Thanks to the cone

I can't gnaw at my stitches

But all these psychological scars

Will never heal

Ponder

· · · · · · · ·

Sometimes

When I'm running on the beach

The warm wind in my face

The cool water at my paws

The bright sun shining on us all

I'll stop for a moment

Look out at the brilliant blue ocean

And think

"Have I really eaten the same exact dinner

For eight years straight?"

Just a Head's Up

. . . .

Every time

Man

Forces one dog

To fight another dog

God

Moves one step closer

To handing the world over to the roaches

I Bite

. . . .

Sometimes I bite when I'm afraid

Sometimes I bite when I'm in pain

Sometimes I bite to protect myself

Sometimes I bite to show I'm in charge

Sometimes I bite because I don't know
   any better

And sometimes I bite because it's been
   four hours

And you're still talking about last night's
   Dancing with the Stars

Sometimes a dog can only take so much

Halloween

. . . .

I don't want to go as a ballerina

For Halloween

Fine, I'll go as a ballerina

If you don't take any photos of me

Fine, you can take one photo of me for Facebook

If I don't have to go outside in this outfit

Fine, I'll go outside in this outfit

If I don't have to be embarrassed
   house to house

Fine, I'll be embarrassed house to house

If I can have some of your chocolate

What do you mean dogs can't have chocolate?

Fine, I'll just eat the wrappers

If I can throw up in your bag

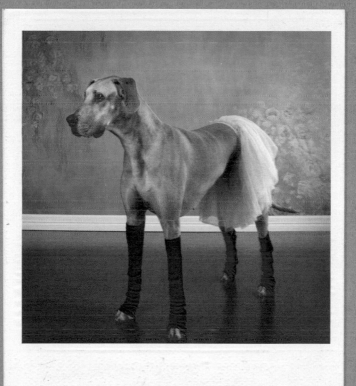

The Best Day

. . . .

Today is the best day

Today is the greatest day

Today is the most amazing

Fantastic

Utterly incredible day

Ever

Because it's Saturday

Wait, it's Tuesday?

Well, that's great, too

3

10

15 16 17

Food

· · · · · ·

Food

Food food food

Food food food food

Food food

Food

Who says a dog

Can't write a love sonnet?

Hello

. . . . . .

I'm sorry he's out of breath

I'm sorry he's in such distress

I'm sorry he's in a fetal position

Sobbing on the floor

But you know if I could

I most certainly would

Give a head's-up by yelling, "CROTCH!"

Before greeting your date full-speed
   at the door

Date Night

· · · · · · · · · · ·

Every time I watch

Lady and the Tramp

I think

"SHE'S HAVING SOME OF YOUR PASTA!"

"QUICK! EAT IT ALL! EAT IT ALL NOW!!!"

"GROWL! BARE YOUR TEETH! DO SOMETHING!"

"OH, DON'T GIVE HER THE MEATBALL!

 THERE'S MEAT IN IT!"

"IDIOT!"

But then again

I'm not the romantic type

Playing

· · · · · · · · ·

We're not fighting

We're playing

We're not arguing

We're playing

We're not biting

We're . . . OW!!!

Really, Mitzi? The thigh?!

Oh, that's it. It's go time!

New Career

. . . .

I think that birds
Should fly high and free
I think that rabbits
Should hop and not flee
I think that ducks
Should swim safe and sound
I think that foxes
Should not fear this hound
I think that as a hunting dog
I should get a new career
So I've been looking through your receipts
And I think I should do your taxes next year

Chasing the Rabbit

· · · · · · · · · · · · · · · · · · · ·

And they're coming around
  the clubhouse turn
And they're coming down the final stretch
And they're coming across the finish line
And Number Five finishes in first place
And Number Five's owner spends his winnings
On hookers and Schlitz
And that is why there are
  no inspirational movies
About dog racing

Treat

. . . .

How long do you

Expect me

To keep

This

Treat

On

My

Nose

Before

I can

GULP

Oh, my bad

Guess we better try this trick a twelfth time

I Could Chew on This

. . . .

Squeak?

Squeak?

Squeak?

Squeak?

How come when I bite down on

this toy it doesn't go "Squeak"?

Maybe because—as you just screamed—

I'm really chewing on your favorite shoe

Or maybe because

I really need to get more of it in my mouth